TREES

A SMALL
APPRECIATION

Lennard Publishing
a division of Lennard Books Ltd
Lennard House
92 Hastings Street
Luton Beds LU1 5BH

British Library Cataloguing in Publication Data

Trees
Poetry in English. Special subjects. Trees. Anthologies

ISBN 1-85291-027-5

First published by Pocknell & Co in December 1987
First issued by Lennard Publishing in April 1988
Copyright © Pocknell & Co 1987

Designed by Pocknell & Co
Printed in England by
Jolly & Barber, Rugby

Although it is now several months since the devastating hurricane of last October, the countryside around my home in Sevenoaks is a constant reminder of the amount of work that still has to be done to repair the damage. The clearance of fallen trees itself will take some time and only then can work begin on the replanting.

This marvellously evocative little book is both a reminder of how much we shall miss those trees that have gone and an encouragement to restore the countryside as quickly as possible. Please buy it and play your small part in helping The Woodland Trust to heal the wound left by the hurricane. Future generations who love this green and pleasant land will forever be indebted to each and every one of you. Thank you.

The living Artists whose work is reproduced here have enthusiastically contributed to our book. Those whose work is published after their death show in their representations the tree's contribution to our landscape and their enthusiasm in representing them.

The Authors speak for themselves.

DAVID POCKNELL

READINGS FARM DECEMBER 1987

Nobody knows what the Wind is,
Under the height of the sky,
Where the hosts of the stars keep far away house
And its wave sweeps by –
Just a great wave of the air,
Tossing the leaves in its sea,
And foaming under the eaves of the roof
That covers me.

JOHN NASH *WASHING LINE*
WALTER DE LA MARE *NOBODY KNOWS PEACOCK PIE*

Here lies a tree which Owl (a bird)
    Was fond of when it stood on end,
    And Owl was talking to a friend
Called Me (in case you hadn't heard)
When something Oo occurred.

For lo! the wind was blusterous
    And flattened out his favourite tree;
    And things looked bad for him and
we –
Looked bad, I mean, for he and us –
I've never known them wuss.

A A. MILNE *THE HOUSE AT POOH CORNER*

S. R. BADMIN

Once, walking home, I passed beneath a Tree,
It filled the air like dark stone statuary,
　　It was so quiet and still,
　　Its thick green leaves a hill
Of strange and faint earth-branching melody.

Over a wall it hung its leaf-starred wood,
And as I lonely there beneath it stood,
　　In that sky-hollow street,
　　Where rang no human feet,
Sweet music flowed and filled me with its flood;

And all my weariness then fell away,
The houses were more lovely than by day;
　　The moon and that old Tree
　　Sang there, and secretly,
With throbbing heart, tiptoe I stole away.

W. J. TURNER *THE MUSIC OF A TREE*

M. COOPER

A fool sees not the same tree that a wise man sees.

WILLIAM BLAKE *THE MARRIAGE OF HEAVEN AND HELL*
PROVERBS OF HELL

TONY EVANS *DEAD ELM AND THE MOON*

The thin night darkens. A breeze from the creased water sighs the streets close under Milk waking Wood. The Wood, whose every tree-foot's cloven in the black glad sight of the hunters of lovers, that is a God-built garden to Mary Ann Sailors who knows there is Heaven on earth and the chosen people of this kind fire in Llaregyb's land, that is the fairday farmhands' wantoning ignorant chapel of bridesbeds, and, to the Reverend Eli Jenkins, a green leaved sermon on the innocence of men, the suddenly wind-shaken wood springs awake for the second dark time this one Spring day.

DYLAN THOMAS *UNDER MILK WOOD*

BRIAN COOK *ENGLISH WOODLAND*

Of all the trees in England,
    Her sweet three corners in,
Only the Ash, the bonnie Ash,
    Burns fierce while it is green.

Of all the trees in England,
    From sea to sea again,
The Willow loveliest stoops her boughs
    Beneath the driving rain.

Of all the trees in England,
    Past frankincense and myrrh,
There's none for smell, of bloom or smoke,
    Like Lime and Juniper.

Of all the trees in England,
    Oak, Elder, Elm and Thorn,
The Yew alone burns lamps of peace
    For them that lie forlorn.

WALTER DE LA MARE *PEACOCK PIE*

JOHN NASH

Some people have what a friend of mine called 'a reserve of likeability', and there are also, I think, some plants which have this quality. The Willows certainly possess it, for the most intimate acquaintance with them does not exhaust their resource of charm, though none of them claim our attention with a surprising beauty.

JASON HILL *THE CONTEMPLATIVE GARDENER*

Tom Purvis NORFOLK

I read, and sigh, and wish I were a tree –
For sure then I should grow
To fruit or shade; at least some bird would trust
Her household to me, and I should be just.

GEORGE HERBERT *THE TEMPLE: 'AFFLICTION'*

JOHN ALDRIDGE

I had a little nut tree
Nothing would it bear
But a silver nutmeg
And a golden pear

The King of Spain's daughter
Came to visit me
All for the sake
Of my little nut-tree.

I skipped over ocean
I danced over sea;
And all the birds in the air
Couldn't catch me.

ANONYMOUS *I HAD A LITTLE NUT TREE*

Below Canal Bridge, on the right bank, grew twelve great trees, with roots awash. Thirteen had stood there – eleven oaks and two ash trees – but the oak nearest the North Star had never thriven, since first a pale green hook had pushed out of a swelled black acorn left by floods on the bank more than three centuries before. In its second year a bullock's hoof had crushed the seedling, breaking its two ruddy leaves, and the sapling grew up crooked. The cleft of its fork held the rains of two hundred years, until frost made a wedge of ice that split the trunk; another century's weather wore it hollow, while every flood took more earth and stones from under it. And one rainy night, when salmon and peal from the sea were swimming against the brown rushing water, the tree had suddenly groaned. Every root carried the groans of the moving trunk, and the voles ran in fear from their tunnels. It rocked until dawn; and when the wind left the land it gave a loud cry, scaring the white owl from its roost, and fell into the river as the sun was rising.

HENRY WILLIAMSON *TARKA THE OTTER*

MARGARET GREEN

Generations pass while some tree stands, and old families last not three oaks.

SIR THOMAS BROWNE *URN BURIAL*

BEN LEVENE *OAK TREE IN CLOUD AND RAIN*

Season of mists and mellow fruitfulness,
Close bosom-friend of the maturing sun;
Conspiring with him how to load and bless
With fruit the vines that round the thatch-eaves run;
To bend with apples the moss'd cottage trees,
And fill all fruit with ripeness to the core;
To swell the gourd and plump the hazel shells
With a sweet kernel, to set budding more,
And still more, later flowers for the bees,
Until they think warm days will never cease,
The summer has o'er-brimmed their clammy cells –

JOHN KEATS *ODE TO AUTUMN*

ROWLAND HILDER

Autumn is over the long leaves that love us,
And over the mice in the barley sheaves;
Yellow the leaves of the rowan above us,
And yellow the wet wild-strawberry leaves.

The hour of the waning of love has beset us,
And weary and worn are our sad souls now;
Let us part, ere the season of passion forget us,
With a kiss and a tear on thy drooping brow.

W. B. YEATS *THE FALLING OF THE LEAVES*

GRAHAM HOGARTH *A LAKELAND FARMHOUSE*

A trusting little leaf of green
A bold audacious frost;
A rendez-vous, a kiss or two,
And youth for ever lost.
Ah, me!
The bitter, bitter cost.

A flaunting patch of bitter red,
That quivers in the sun;
A windy gust, a grove of dust,
The little race is run.
Ah, me!
Were that the only one.

ELLA WHEELER WILCOX *A FALLEN LEAF*

BEN LEVENE *SNOW*

Youthful lovers in my shade
Their vows of truth and rapture made;
And on my trunk's surviving frame,
Carved many a long forgotten name.

RICHARD ST. BARBE BAKER *FAMOUS TREES*

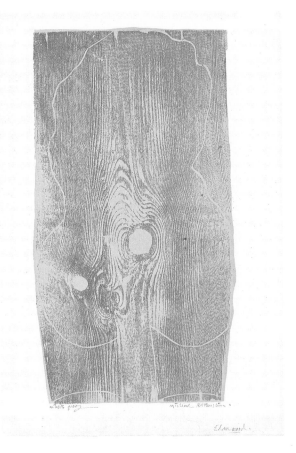

artist's proof —   Michael Rothenstein

Elmwood.

MICHAEL ROTHENSTEIN *ELMWOOD*

It was a world of glass, sparkling and motionless.
Vapours had frozen all over the trees and transformed
them into confections of sugar.

LAURIE LEE *CIDER WITH ROSIE*

RUSKIN SPEAR *SNOW IN RICHMOND PARK*

A north-country maid up to London had stray'd
Although with her nature it did not agree;
She wept, and she sigh'd, and she bitterly cried,
I wish once again in the north I could be.
"Oh! the oak, and the ash, and the bonny ivy tree,
They flourish at home in my own country."

TRADITIONAL NORTH COUNTRY *OH! THE OAK AND THE ASH*

PETER BLAKE *THE OLD OAK TREE*

He walked through the garden door, now left open, through which Arabella had gone. She was standing beneath a huge cedar, looking up into the sky. She looked like a contemporary immortal – if there could be such a creature – her hair streaming farther down her back with her upturned head, the white crepe clinging and flowing when she moved. She had kicked off her shoes, and they lay tossed upon the lawn. The lawn had not been cut for some time – it was covered with daisies and clover and the odd buttercup, except where she stood under the great, dark tree. Beyond her stretched more lawns studded with trees at graceful intervals. He thought she had not seen him, but before he could stop watching her, she said:

'There's a broken down old greenhouse with a lot of grapes. Mildewed, though. Shall we explore?'

'I must do the house first, I'm afraid.'

ELIZABETH JANE HOWARD *ODD GIRL OUT*

PETER COKER *LA MAISON ROUGE JARDIN*

We would like to thank all the generous contributors to this book.
In particular, Peter Blake for finishing his drawing so that we could print it!

No book on trees would be complete without the work of Stanley Badmin and
we thank both the artists and Chris Beetles for permission to reproduce his
illustrations from the Dropmore Press edition of 'Trees' by
Richard St Barbe Baker.

Permissions have been received from the following publishers and authors and
we are indebted to them for their promptness.

'The House At Pooh Corner,' by A A Milne, published by Methuen Children's
Books, reproduced by permission of Curtis Brown, London.
'Nobody Knows' and 'Trees' from Peacock Pie reproduced by permission of The
Literary Trustees of Walter De La Mare and The Society of Authors as their
representatives.
Extract from 'Cider With Rosie' by Laurie Lee reproduced by permission of the
author and Hogarth Press.
Extract from 'The Contemplative Gardener' by Jason Hill reproduced by kind
permission of Mrs Jill Leech.
Extract from 'Under Milk Wood' by Dylan Thomas reproduced by permission of
the Trustees for the estate of Dylan Thomas, and J M Dent & Son, Publishers.
'English Woodland' by Brian Cook from 'The Britain of Brian Cook' published
by Batsford.
Extract from 'Odd Girl Out' by Elizabeth Jane Howard reproduced by
permission of the author and Jonathan Cape Publishers.
We apologise to those people whom we have been unable to trace for
permission before going to print.

Special thanks to Jigsaw Graphics, Typesetters, Romford; Michael Leitch,
Bruce and Paul for their help in compiling this book.